This Book Belongs To:

....

....

Copyright 2021 by Sunshine Creations. All Rights Reseved

Written and Published by: Sunshine Creations
Illustrated by: Ali Pouraza

Shoofully Discovers the Wind

One day Ben and his mom decided to take me on a car ride, even though I was comfortable lying on a square of sunshine on the living room floor.

Ben put my collar and leash on, and we were ready to leave.

I'm getting pretty good at walking on a leash, and I really enjoy going for walks with Ben.

I didn't realize that I've been running so fast, that Ben had gotten scratches on his knees trying to keep up with me in the bushes.

Suddenly someone lifted me up from the ground! It was Ben's mom. She turned me around and looked all over my body.

Then she did the same thing with Ben!
"Ben, you have scratches on your knees and Shoofully has gotten burrs on his paws. Let's go back inside" she said.

We went back in, and Ben's mom washed Ben's tiny scratches with clean water and took out the burrs from my paws.

As she was doing all that, she was telling Ben that I am very young, and I might get too excited about any noise or smell, and then I might get into trouble. She told Ben to be more careful.

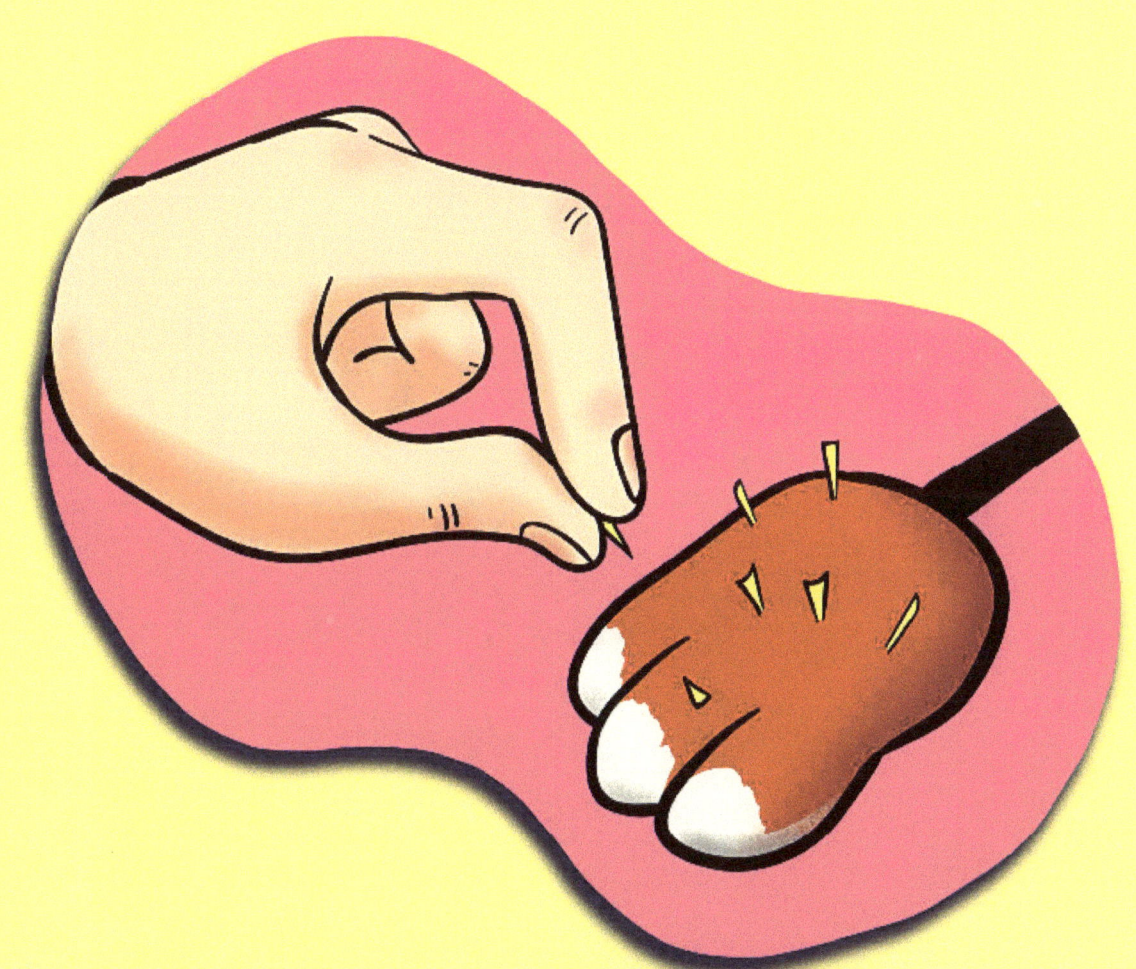

Then turned to me, scratched my neck and said: "Oh! You little trouble!" and then laughed. I love Ben's mom.

It was a nice sunny day.
We got in to the car and
Ben rolled down the window.

I stuck my head out. We started moving and
the wind started running through my fur.
Ben was holding me really tight.
I felt safe and happy

I turned my head and licked his face.
He laughed. I laughed too.
In my own way, you know.

And then something else happened.
I think I got too excited again and oops!!
I did a little tinkly on Ben's shorts.
I was so confused! I don't know how it happened.

Ben said.

We had to go back home for the second time,
so that Ben could change his shorts.
I was a little sorry but I got to stick my
head out of the window again on the way back.

My ears were flopping in the air, and I bet I looked really funny because kids in other cars were pointing at me and laughing.

Seems like I've been a handful today but at least I made a lot of kids laugh, right?

Ben gave me a delicious chewy and told me to wait in the car.
Then he pulled down the window a little bit and closed the door.

I was in the car all by myself.
I finished the chewy and I was getting bored

I thought I can put my head close to the window
and play with the wind again.
But there was no wind.

Did the wind go to the supermarket too?

So, I started calling them. I was barking when I saw Ben and his mom walking towards the car.

So, I barked even louder to help them find me!
I was really helpful!

Today other than learning about the wind
(apparently, wind only shows up when the car is moving),
I realized that Ben doesn't know how to bark!
So, I'm trying to find other ways to talk to him.
It's going to be fun!

Follow us on Facebook or Instagram to find out what happens to Shoofully next!
You will be the first to know when the next book is ready to be published.

Check us out in Instagram and Facebook:

 Facebook.com/sunshinecreations555

 Instegram.com/sunshinecreations555

Email us at: sunshinecreations555@Gmail.com

Check out Book #1 & 2 in my Amazon author page

amazon.com/author/sunshinecreations555

www.ingramcontent.com/pod-product-compliance
Lightning Source LLC
Chambersburg PA
CBHW051305110526
44589CB00025B/2945